Who Am I?

Figure Out YOUR Identity

Zohra Sarwari

Eman Publishing
P.O. Box 404
FISHERS, IN 46038

www.emanpublishing.com

Order Online: www.zohrasarwari.com

ISBN 13: 978-0-9823125-9-9
ISBN 10: 0-9823125-9-8
LCCN: 2009902381

EMAN
publishing

Cover Design by Zeeshan Shaikh

Printed in the United States of America

Who Am I?

Figure Out YOUR Identity

Zohra Sarwari

Dedication

'(Our Lord! Accept this from us. You are All-Hearing, the All-Knowing).'

(The Qur'aan: Chapter 2, Verse 127)

Acknowledgments

In the name of Allaah (SWT), the Most Gracious, the Most Magnificent. All praise is due to Allaah (SWT), Lord of the universe. We praise Him, seek His help and His forgiveness, and we seek His protection from the accursed Satan. Whomever Allaah (SWT) guides will never be misguided, and whomever He allows to be misguided will never be guided. I bear witness that there is no deity worthy of worship except Allaah (SWT), who is One; alone, and has no partners. I bear witness that Muhammad (PBUH) is His servant and messenger. May the blessings of Allaah (SWT) be upon him, his family, his companions and the righteous that follow them until the Day of Judgment.

I would like to thank my family and friends for all of their support, especially Zeeshan, Madeeha, and Saqib Sheikh who are an asset to my team *masha'Allaah*. A very special thanks goes to Dr. Daoud Nassimi for all of his efforts and hard work in reviewing, editing, and providing feedback about this book. *Jazaakum-Allaahu khayran* - May Allaah (SWT) reward you all - ameen!

Table of Contents

Chapter

1

Discover
Your Identity

'Accepting who you are is the first step to success, insha'Allaah.'

Zohra Sarwari

What is 'Teen Identity'? I have realized this is one of the most powerful questions presented to teens. As a teen, I thought I knew everything; I knew more than my parents and other adults in some matters; and the matters in which I felt my knowledge was weak, I thought I can learn more than them *insha'Allaah*. For all of you who are reading this, how many of you can relate to what I am saying? Do you agree? Lol . . . I know you're laughing and most likely saying "Yes".

'Teen Identity' is when a youth must go through several developmental stages to figure out who they are. By this age, most teens have a good foundation of knowledge, but they are trying to discover where they fit in. 'Who am I?' is the question that is most asked. What's more interesting is when teens try to identify who they want to become; this can be a time of empowerment or loss. Some teens have great role models to look up to, while others don't.

Some of you might want to explore new things and this can be scary for you and your parents. I suggest one way to curb this appetite is by getting yourself involved in activities that stimulate your brain, as well as enhance your social life; some activities I would suggest are, study circles, karate, and other sports that may interest you, etc. This will be even better for you if you attend it with like-minded individuals; for instance other Muslim friends. This will strengthen your identity of who you are and which path is best for you. Remember that whilst doing such activities you are still responsible for how you dress and act.

As a teen you may be going through changes; they may be physical, emotional and/or psychological. Your body will change, your dress sense may change, your social life might change; you could make new friends and lose old friends, you might have new ideas, you may wish to mingle with the opposite gender, etc. Going through some of these changes makes one try to sort out what it is that you believe in; what are your values and goals? There are so many changes one goes through and this can be overwhelming. Yet it is at this time that you want to discover and fit in somewhere; be someone.

Identity Development

So you're a teen and want to know what type of changes you may go through until you finally discover your identity. Here is a list; Warning! These may not necessarily apply to you; these are just the typical issues that most teens face. I will discuss five issues that teens might come across:

1. Status symbols
2. Rebellion
3. Human idols
4. Forbidden behaviors
5. Cliques

What does it mean to have status symbols? This is when teens will wear some type of brand names to show who they are. They want to drive certain cars only; wear certain types of sunglasses etc; these types of symbols identify the teen without really being in any clique. It just shows who they are by their outer appearance. Many teens go through this phase (if they have the money to do it); they will beg their parents for the Polo shirt, or Nike sneakers, just so that they feel like they are amongst the status quo. They feel it means something to people and they want to feel significant.

Rebellious acts, who didn't know this one? Lol . . . This is something that most teens go through. This is when teens defy the adults in order to be accepted by their peers; they want to show that they are not like their parents, by doing things in a different way, even if it's the wrong way! For example, some kids want to get bad grades just so they are identified as different from their smart parents. Authority is not something they enjoy; they feel they don't need laws to hold them back; they can figure things out on their own. Fortunately deep down most teens know that this is wrong and that they have to change; the only problem is how long will pass before they actually change. If you're a teen and you're going through this you should do something that will outperform teens in a good way. You will get lots of attention this way and you will be happy with yourself. A great place to start is reading the book, *'9 Steps To Achieve Your Destiny'*. This book was designed for youth to learn how to discover the gold that is within them. So often our youth are neglected in this area and yet they have more guts and energy to make it happen than most adults. Get the book and find a different way to rebel!

By having some kind of idols to imitate, teens feel great. Usually the idols will be movie stars, singers, or someone they can relate to. Teens, this can be very dangerous for you, because what may look like a lifestyle you want, can actually be very deceiving. Real life is not a show, it's different and unfortunately most celebrities put on a show for us, as that is what they get paid for. If you are about to pick a role model, think hard and be wise about who you really want to be; make sure that your role models truly reflect you. Remember, *"All that glistens is not gold!"* As Muslims we have great role models such as the Prophet Muhammad (PBUH), the Sahaabah, Maryam (PBUH) (mother of Jesus (PBUH)), Khadijah (RA), 'Aishah (RA), and many more, *alhamdulillaah*. Take these great role models who were true inside out and make them your role models. They were consistent all the time and that is how we should be. I would suggest reading their biographies, and finding out who these great people were.

The fourth category can get a bit dangerous when teens want to show who they are through forbidden behaviors. If you're a teen and you're reading this, you know what I am talking about; smoking, drugs, drinking, free mixing with the opposite gender, etc; anything that really isn't good for you, but you see adults doing it, therefore you feel if you do it, you will be recognized as an adult. I am here to give you one piece of advice as a sister, DON'T DO IT! It actually lowers everyone's respect for you and it shows people that you aren't strong enough in your personality and that you are trying to be someone you are not. These behaviors can come from many places; from peer pressure, from trying to fit in at work, from hanging around older people, etc. This is why I think it is so important to be working on the genius within you and build yourself to be the best, so that you're not a follower; you're a leader instead. Instead of copying others, you become so great by the Will of Allaah (SWT) that other people want to imitate you. This is what you need; a new perspective on life *insha'Allaah*.

Lastly, some teens think that by being in certain cliques or groups they are better than everybody else. NO! I love my teens and I know how it feels to be one, but I will be honest, cliques don't make you a better person, your actions make you a better person; who you are, what you stand for, your morals, your character. In fact the group you become a part of can hurt you instead of helping you.

A quote to remember is what Henry Ford said, *"Whether you think you can, or think you can't, you're right."* Often we think we can't do that, or we can't be this way, but that is just the shaytaan whispering in your head. *Insha'Allaah* you can do it; all you need to do is try, and never give up. Remember my sisters and brothers, you are very special but you're also very vulnerable in many ways at this stage in your life. Don't let this be your weakness. Use your inner strength that Allaah (SWT) has blessed you with to become great and make a difference in this world for the sake of Allaah (SWT). Remember that Allaah (SWT) created all of us, and to think that we are better than someone else is wrong. Instead we should think about how we can help others who need help in finding themselves. So if we can focus on doing our best, then we can also focus on helping others become their best as well, *insha'Allaah*.

Muslim Dress Code

A lot of teens ask me this question, *"Zohra, how are we to dress? Everyone has a different explanation as to how we should dress. Some say one thing while other Muslims say another; please explain?"*
I tell them that, *"This is one of my favorite questions and that they are smart for even asking."* Most teens become quiet and are afraid to speak to people who they think are knowledgeable or even smarter than them; they are embarrassed to look bad or even dumb. I want to address all my sisters and brothers who live in the West about this subject; how one should be dressing as a Muslim sister or brother. I will go over **4 important things** every *Muslimah* (female Muslim) should know about the best way to dress, and then I will discuss what every brother should know, *insha'Allaah*:

1. The *Muslimah* should be covering her body and hair in front of any man who is not her brother, father,

maternal uncle, paternal uncle, grandparent, nephew, husband.

Allaah (SWT) says in the Qur'aan in Surah al-Ahzaab, ayah 59:

> "Oh Prophet, tell your wives and your daughters and the women of the believers to draw their outer garments close around them. That will be better, that they may be known and so not be bothered. And Allaah is Oft-Forgiving, Most Merciful."

Abu Dawood recorded that 'A'ishah (RA) said:

> 'Asma came to see the Messenger of Allaah (PBUH). She was wearing a thin dress; the Prophet (PBUH) turned away from her and said to her: "O Asma, once a woman reaches the age of puberty no part of her body should be uncovered except her face and hands."'

Ibn 'Umar narrated:

> 'The Prophet (PBUH) said: "On the Day of Judgment Allaah will not look upon one who trails his garment along out of pride." Umm Salamah then asked: "What should women do with their garments?" The Prophet (PBUH) said: "They may lower them a hand span." She said: "Their feet would still be

uncovered." The Prophet (PBUH) said: then lower them a forearm's length, but no more."

(Abu Dawood and Tirmidhi)

2. The outer garment must be thick enough to conceal the clothes worn under it and loose enough to conceal the woman's form. Wearing tight clothes but saying that it is covering everything does not make it okay. There are a few *ahadith* that address this matter:

The Prophet (PBUH) said:

> "There will be, in the last days of my Ummah (nation), women who are dressed and yet undressed. Curse them: they are accursed."

(At-Tabarani)

Abu Hurairah related that the Prophet (PBUH) referred to:

> "...women who are naked even though they are wearing clothes, go astray and make others go astray, and they will not enter paradise nor smell its fragrance, although it can be smelled from afar."

(At-Tabarani)

Think about it; in one sense you're dressed, but the clothes that you're wearing are revealing your body and exposing it. You're basically telling yourself its okay, but really you know that one of the purposes behind the way you have dressed is to get attention, to fit in, to be seen, etc.

The Prophet (PBUH) said:

> *"Belief and modesty are tied together; if one is lost the other is lost."*

(Al-Hakim)

3. The *Muslimah* should not wear perfume in public.

The Prophet (PBUH) said:

> *"Any woman who wears perfume then goes out to the mosque, so that the fragrance can be discerned, her prayers will not be accepted until she performs ghusl like the ghusl to be performed when in a state of janaabah."*

(Reported by Imaam Ahmad, 2/444; see also Saheeh al-Jaami', 2703)

I want you to think about the *ahadith* that you just read. If it is inappropriate for us to attend the mosque wearing perfume, then how much more inappropriate is it to where it anywhere else? You may ask why we can't wear perfume. The answer is, because scent attracts attention to a woman and may thereby stimulate low desires in the opposite gender. This is wrong no matter where you are, whether that is the mosque, shopping center, school, work, etc.

I want to advise my young sisters, that while perfume is only allowed to be worn in an all women's gathering, or around *mahram* men in the family, deodorant can be used anywhere *insha'Allaah*. It's okay to smell clean, you don't need to use perfume odor deodorants, just the plain ones that won't make you smell like sweat.

4. The *Muslimah's* clothes should not resemble men's clothing.

Abu Hurairah said that the Messenger of Allaah (PBUH) said,

"Allaah curses a woman who wears men's clothing and a man who wears a woman's dress."

(Abu Dawood)

Ibn 'Umar said that he heard the Messenger of Allaah (PBUH) say:

"He is not of us who imitates women nor is she of us who imitates men (in appearance)."

(Al Hakim)

If you can follow these four things, then *insha'Allaah* you're on your way sisters, to becoming the best *Muslimahs*!

Remember this ayah and what Allaah (SWT) tells us:

He says in Surah al-Ahzaab, ayah 59:

> *'Oh Prophet, tell your wives and your daughters and the women of the believers to draw their outer garments close around them.* ***That will be better, that they may be known and so not be bothered.*** *And Allaah is Oft-Forgiving, Most Merciful.'*

Insha'Allaah I hope my teen sisters understand the awesome dress code for the awesome *Muslimah*. Now let me address the teen brothers:

1. We already know that the men's clothing must not resemble the women's clothing and vice versa.

2. Silk clothing is prohibited for the Muslim man:

Narrated Hudhaifa:

"The Prophet forbade us to drink out of gold and silver vessels, or eat in it. And also forbade the wearing of silk and Dibaj, or sitting on it."

(Bukhari, Volume 7, Book 72)

"The Prophet ordered us to observe seven things: To visit the sick; follow funeral processions; say 'May Allaah bestow His Mercy on you', to the sneezer if he says, 'Praise be to Allaah! He forbade us to wear silk, Dibaj, Qassiy and Istibarq (various kinds of silken clothes); or to use red Mayathir (silk-cushions)." (See Hadith No. 253 A, Vol. 8)

(Bukhari Volume 7, Book 72)

3. Men and women are forbidden to wear clothing that are dragging or hanging low due to conceit or pride:

Narrated 'Abdullaah bin 'Umar:

"The Prophet (PBUH) said Allaah will not look on the Day of Resurrection at the person who drags his garment (behind him) out of conceit. On that Abu Bakr said, 'O Allaah's Apostle! One side of my izar hangs low if I do not take care of it.' The Prophet (PBUH) said, 'You are not one of those who do that out of conceit.'"

(Sahih Bukhari, Volume 7, Book 72)

4. Gold is also prohibited for men to wear:

Allaah (SWT) has prohibited two kinds of adornment for men, while permitting them to women; gold ornaments and clothing made of pure silk.

"Ali reported that the Prophet (peace be on him) took some silk in his right hand and some

gold in his left, declaring, 'These two are haram for the males among my followers.'"

(Reported by Ahmad, Abu Dawood, an-Nisai, Ibn Hayyan, and Ibn Majah, who reports the additional phrase, *"but halal for the females."***)**

"Umar reported that he heard the Prophet (peace be on him) say, 'Do not wear silk, for those who wear it in this life shall not wear it in the Hereafter.'"

(Bukhari and Muslim)

5. Lastly, I would say the brothers need to be modest in their dress as well. They need to know that if they are wearing clothing just to impress the opposite gender that might not be the best thing to do. Intentions are everything; our intention for everything should be: does it please Allaah (SWT)?

It is narrated on the authority of 'Umar ibn al-Khattab, *radiyallaahu 'anhu*, who said: I heard the Messenger of Allaah, *sallallaahu 'alayhi wasallam*, say:

"Actions are (judged) by motives (niyyah), so each man will have what he intended. Thus, he whose migration (hijrah) was to Allaah and His Messenger, his migration is to Allaah and His Messenger; but he whose migration was for some worldly thing he might gain, or for a wife

he might marry, his migration is to that for which he migrated."

(Bukhari and Muslim)

Activity to do

I want you to write down your story of self identity; write down 5 things you have discovered about yourself and 5 things you have changed about your personality to develop it in a positive way, but still manage to enjoy your teen self.

Chapter

2

Teen Self-Esteem

'Be confident, but not arrogant.'

Zohra Sarwari

What is Self-Esteem? Let's define this word before we discuss the power of it *insha'Allaah*:

Self - is YOU

Esteem - is to have high regard for something or someone.

When one has high self-esteem they are happy with themselves; they like themselves for who they are and they like what they look like. Most of the time, one does feel like this when for instance we pass a hard test or do something that we didn't think was accomplishable or was extremely difficult. When people praise you your self-esteem rises; when people criticize you your self-esteem declines.

Having high self-esteem is vital to one's success, but most teens don't like everything about themselves. As a matter of fact, most teens always look at their negative aspects rather than their positive aspects. This is a growing phenomenon all over the world; to complain about what you are bad at; your grades aren't good enough, you are overweight, you don't like how you look, etc. This is called low self-esteem.

Whether you have high self-esteem or low self-esteem it is something that you have gotten over time from other people; think about it, what your parents, siblings, family, teachers said about you, is what you started to believe about yourself. If you got good reactions from them, then most likely your self-esteem is high. If however you got bad reactions from them then most likely your self-esteem will be low. Self-esteem is also built on what you see on TV and magazines; when you see certain people dressing a certain way and you start to look like them, your self-esteem also gets built.

Most teens struggle with their self-esteem when they hit puberty. One of the reasons for this is that they are going through so many changes in their body. With these changes and having a natural desire to be 'accepted', is when teens begin to compare themselves with others. Again comparison could take place with their peers or celebrities they see on TV, in movies, or magazines. As a teen you must remember that the changes that come with puberty are different for everyone; some people's voice changes, while others don't, some people fill out, while others get a growth spurt, etc.

As a Muslim teen, I want to tell you the importance of self-esteem relating to your identity, *insha'Allaah*. First, and foremost, your self-esteem should only rise when you're obeying Allaah (SWT). This is important to understand, because your parents, teachers, or friends might not care about this, so they will put you down. Does it mean you need them to praise you? No! On the other hand, obeying your parents in everything else they ask you as long as it doesn't go against Allaah (SWT) is essential . . . *insha'Allaah*. Actually obeying them on other matters such as: asking you to do something for them, taking them shopping, helping them in any way, etc, should be respected and handled with patience.

Why is it important to have high self-esteem? The most important reason is that you now have more responsibility to choose between right and wrong. Your parents are not always with you. If you have positive self-esteem then you will have the courage to be who you are regardless of the situation you are in. You won't be worried to say 'no' to things that don't involve you. You will have a sense of who you are as a Muslim. For example, you don't drink alcohol, you can say that; you don't celebrate Christmas, you can say that. You have developed who you are, and are not afraid to be yourself *insha'Allaah*. Think for yourself; don't let your friends think for you, only you know what is right for you, so why are you letting others make you do something you don't want to do, or something that is wrong to do. Muslims know that on the Day of Judgment they will be responsible for all of their actions, not their friends. Think about all that you do before you do it and think about how you will answer for it.

Also having high self-esteem helps you influence how you live your life; think about it, if you're happy with your life then you will be happy in your relationships and how you treat others. You're also not afraid to ask for help and support if you should need it. This in turn allows you to solve more problems, and accomplish more goals *insha'Allaah*.

Activity to do

The next question many teens ask me is *'How do you get high self-esteem if you don't have it?'* I will give you an exercise to do now. Make a list of all the things that you're not happy with about you.

Once you have done this, I want you to set realistic goals for yourself. Next I want you to work on some areas that you can to be good enough so that you're happy with yourself. For example, you want to go to college, make sure that your Grade Point Average is at least a 2.5 or higher to be able to get into some of the state schools. This gives you confidence that you have a chance, but also if you were to work a bit harder, you can get into a better school, and possibly get a scholarship. Remember to not compare yourself to anyone, when looking at the worldly life, but compare yourself only in the race of earning good deeds. You can only be the best you, not the best someone else.

Allaah (SWT) has given each of us different strengths and weaknesses. You must begin to understand what your strengths and weaknesses are, and who you are, *insha'Allaah*.

Another example for many of the sisters here is weight. If weight is an issue that you have that is making your self-esteem low, look into eating healthier and exercising. By tackling the areas in which we want to change our self for the better, our self-esteem will tend to rise *insha'Allaah*, and we will tend to be more confident about who we are.

Activity to do

The next activity is to write down all the things that you're good at. Celebrate your achievements, by saying *"Alhamdulillaah."* (All Praise is for Allaah, the Creator who has given you this talent).

Chapter

3

Teen
Time-Management

'You only have a limited amount of time on Earth, so make the most of it.'

Zohra Sarwari

Is there such a thing as teen time-management? Lol! Some would probably say yes and others would probably say no to this. Let me ask you a different question; how do many teens join sports, get straight A's, work part-time, help out with chores and manage to be happy? This is called teen time-management. Teen time-management is a skill that is taught, not something that teens are born with. Most skills are taught and mastered through time. However, if you are like most teens, you don't know how to do this just yet, and it is a skill that was not taught to you by your parents. Let me tell you, if you can master juggling many hats, then you will excel and grow much faster in all that you do.

How can a teen manage his/her time? I have devised a system called, *"Anybody Can Do It!"* *insha'Allaah*. It consists of 4 steps which teach you how to manage your time and be the most productive *insha'Allaah*.

Step 1: **Make A List** of all the important things that you must get done. This includes homework assignments, tests to study for, events to prepare for, family-time, sports or extracurricular activities, and work. Once you know what is important to you then you prioritize your list. Studies should be number one.

After that depending on how long other activities take, I would suggest no more than 3 extracurricular activities a week. Personally, I think with homework and studying, one extracurricular activity a day should be enough. For example,

- Monday, Tuesday and Wednesday - *haafiz* program to memorize the Qur'aan;

- Thursday and Saturday - go to karate classes;

- Friday night - is *halaqah* (study circles) at the Masjid, and family night;

- Saturday and Sunday - work 5 hours per day (babysitting, helping parents, tutoring, etc).

- As you can tell, by now you're pretty busy!

Step 2: Get Organized. Prepare ahead of time. Always plan ahead your activities and studies, *insha'Allaah*. Prepare your lesson for memorization ahead of time; prepare your clothes ahead of time, etc; you know what you will need, so get it ready the day or night before. Lastly, if you're organized then you can enjoy your "Free Time". Free time is when you get to do something fun for you; you can read a book, start a side business, go to the park with your friends and family, draw, listen to lectures, etc.

Step 3: Make It Happen! This is the part that most teens have problems with. They know what must get done, but just get bogged down by the small tasks.

They also get stressed about all the stuff that they have to do, which means they don't even begin to do anything. This puts everything on the back burner and stress begins to pile up. Now that you know what you need to do, just do it. This can be the hardest step for most teens; DOING the actual tasks. Yet this is the most important step; MAKING IT HAPPEN! This is where you must push yourself; when your energy is decreasing and you want to stop, just give yourself one extra push, *insha'Allaah*, it will be worth it in the end!

Step 4: **Turn It Into A Habit:** If you work on this pattern for several weeks *insha'Allaah,* and actually abide by your schedule, you will notice it pretty soon. Then you realize you can add other things to your schedule as well and still be successful *insha'Allaah*.

Activity to do

Please answer the questions below:

Step 1: Write a list of all the important things that you need to get done?

Step 2: What do you need to get organized?

Step 3: What do you need to 'make happen'?

Step 4: What do you want to turn into a habit?

School Time-Management

So many people want to know how they can manage their time with school, on a daily basis. I gave some tips for teen time-management and now I will be specific with what you should do as a teen with a school schedule:

1. I highly recommend getting a schedule book for all of your homework assignments, tests and other projects for school. Since school comes first, you want to be organized as much as you possibly can *insha'Allaah*. Next, you need to make sure that you have some folders for your different classes; this way the important papers that are given to you go into each important folder, so that you do not lose them when you need them, *insha'Allaah*.

2. I highly recommend scheduling a time for doing homework and studying. For example, 4 pm to 6 pm is studying time. You focus on doing all of your subjects at that time. Something else I HIGHLY recommend, is trying to do homework during breaks, and while you're waiting for the teacher to start the daily lessons, or when you're done with your work in class. This will help cut out a lot of wasted time and help you be more productive, *insha'Allaah*. Make sure that you tell everyone in your family about your new schedule, so that they don't bother you, unless it is prayer time or something very important.

3. I highly recommend that when you're doing something, do your best. This means you cannot be distracted by other things happening in the background; you can't have your phone buzzing with messages, your TV on, babysitting, the internet, etc. You need to be alone, in a space where you can focus on what you have to get done. If you have your own room, that would be great. If not, then maybe you could go to the library to get your work done *insha'Allaah*.

4. I highly recommend talking about your assignments to your parents or someone older that may be able to help you and also understand what you're dealing with. This helps others sympathize with your workload *insha'Allaah*.

5. I highly recommend you to break your big projects and tests into small weekly projects. As humans we tend to procrastinate until the last minute and then get stressed out that it is too difficult to do. If it is in smaller chunks and worked on a daily or weekly basis for 10 minutes a day then it won't be so bad in the end *insha'Allaah*.

Chapter

4

Teen Intelligence

'The more you use your mind, the wiser you become, insha'Allaah.'

Zohra Sarwari

What is teen intelligence? Teen intelligence means teen smarts and teen knowledge. This is a word that I have made up . . . I figured that teens are very smart *masha'Allaah,* and that they need their own term for intelligence. For one to have teen intelligence one must be thinking with their brain. It doesn't mean that you need straight A's to be smart; grades are important but they aren't the only factor to determine your true intelligence. Your true intelligence depends on many other factors. I have come up with a formula for teen intelligence, it has 3 factors that weigh in together to make it a whole; Teen School Smarts, Teen Street Smarts and Teen Islam Smarts.

1. Teen School Smarts

We all know what 'Teen School Smarts' means; when one is smart in their studies in school. This includes subjects such as Math, Reading, History, Science, English, Language Arts, etc; this is where teens spend most of their time. He or she is in school learning for the majority of the day and then at home doing homework for those same classes. Many teens are successful in this area in the sense that they attain grades A's, B's and some C's, which means they are learning most of the stuff that is being taught to them. It is important to study and learn studying skills because these skills will and can be used in real life examples. I definitely recommend to study as much as you can and learn as much as you can. When you love to learn, then your grades will be the best, *insha'Allaah.*

I will give you some advice in this area to help you improve your grades and become the best student you can be *insha'Allaah.* I want you to remember as I am teaching you these skills that they are not just for high school; these are skills that you should use throughout your life, in all spheres of your life *insha'Allaah.*

Remember that learning never ends; if you stop learning, then you stop growing to be better and better each day *insha'Allaah.* Think about learning as a bank account, every time you study, you deposit some gold in it; eventually the gold becomes so much that you start to share the gold with others. When you begin to do this, you can become very wealthy because people will pay for your knowledge *insha'Allaah,* and you'll realize that it pays to study and learn!

Successful Study Skills:

1. ***Dream about what you want to be, insha'Allaah.*** Dream big here; imagine that you are a scholar, a haafiz, a doctor, an engineer and then know that there are steps you must take to be able to achieve your dream. This is where most people stop; they

give up for they think to achieve this dream one must have special skills, knowledge and money. While all of this is true to an extent, what you forget is, that to achieve your dreams you need one ingredient and the willingness to work hard no matter what; that ingredient is PASSION. If you have the passion to be anything you dream of, then don't give up on it. Keep working on it and your dreams will come true, *insha'Allaah*.

2. ***Be a Decision-Maker!*** Know that in order for you to succeed YOU need to make decisions about your priorities as well as your time.

3. ***Studying can be a form of worshiping Allaah (SWT)!*** For Muslims, any action can be counted as an act of worship of Allaah (SWT) as long as the intention is to please our Lord; the action is permissible in Islam; and as long as one has done the obligatory acts of worship. Therefore, studying for school can form an act of worship for a practicing Muslim student. When you think of your life this way it's as if you're constantly getting credit to learn to help yourself in this world as well as the hereafter. This is the power of thought! It can also be very motivating to keep you going when you want to quit and give up. Don't let people tell you what is important to you when you already know it yourself.

4. ***Be productive by waking up early, and sleeping early!*** When can you get a lot of work done? This is vital for you to know and understand. Again, for Muslims the early hours in the morning have the most *barakah* (blessings). I have personally tried and tested this theory. I used to think I was a night person, until I read this and then heard Anthony Robbins and other gurus confirm this theory. *Masha'Allaah* I changed my sleeping pattern to sleeping after Isha prayer, and waking up at about 5 am; beginning my day with prayers and then getting to work.

5. ***Find at least 3 different ways to be able to solve your problems!*** Many times we read something and can't understand it. If you can't understand what you're reading or how to do your project, then look for another way to understand it; ask a teacher, ask your parents, ask a classmate, get a tutor. There are a 100 different ways to bake cookies and that is what I want you to figure out.

2. Teen Street Smarts

This is my favorite section of the book, I always test people to see if they are street smart, and so many times I realize people are intelligent in books but not on the street. What does 'Street Smart' mean? Being 'street smart' means knowing how to keep yourself safe while with other kids, or when you're alone outside.

When you're street smart, you usually know how to handle yourself in difficult situations, and you're able to read people. This is a great skill for everyone to learn, not just teens, but adults as well. I will be going over a list of <u>ten powerful things</u> that all teens should know to be *Super Street Smart*.

1. **<u>Trust YOUR instincts;</u>** this is usually your gut feeling telling you that someone or something is wrong. If you feel this way, then you need to avoid that person and/or situation.

2. **<u>Always take the safest routes to school and home;</u>** where there is plenty of lighting and a safe place to go in case of an emergency.

3. **<u>Don't accept anything from anyone you don't know;</u>** this includes rides, food, money, etc. Strangers usually tamper with food and it can harm you more than it can help you. This includes people that you meet from the internet, mall and anywhere else.

4. **<u>Be alert at all times;</u>** keep your eyes and ears open and be aware of your surroundings.

5. **<u>Have your keys close by;</u>** find your keys and keep them in your hand, before you reach the car or the house; this way you can get in quickly, instead of looking for them by the car or the house while nervous.

6. Don't answer the door when you're alone; this is vital to remember! Do not open the door to strangers when you're alone. Call your parents or the police if someone is insisting on coming into your house.

7. Never be alone when you are outside; always try to go out with your family or a group of friends, this is especially important for girls.

8. CALL 911; Yell, should someone try to attack you. This is a clear message to anyone who can hear to 'call 911'. This indicates that an emergency is taking place, while alerting people around you to help you.

9. Know basic self-defense; Take a class on how to handle someone who attacks you from different positions. This is excellent for all ages. Predators can go after anyone.

10. Don't display your money or jewelry; to act cool; many teens like to show off what they have. This can be dangerous to you because someone might attack you for what you have.

11. The biggest weapon that you have is *du'aa*! *Du'aa* is the weapon of a believer. Always recite *Ayatul Kursi* wherever you are. I would also recommend the *du'aa* that one recites before one leaves the home, and any other *surahs* you have memorized.

3. Teen Islam Smarts

This is where one must be smart in the basics of Islam. I will name eleven *'Teen Islam Smarts'* and I want you to post them in your room *insha'Allaah*. These eleven 'Teen Islam Smarts' are for you to memorize and tell others about, *insha'Allaah*. Every teen should know it in this order and should explain it to others in this order, *insha'Allaah*:

1. *Worshiping Allaah alone, and obeying Him*: The single most important thing for every Muslim teen to never forget is that we believe in One, and Only ONE God; the Creator of the heavens and the earth. Remember that we are on this earth to worship Him and Him alone.

'And your Ilâh (God) is One Ilâh (God - Allâh), Lâ ilâha illa Huwa (there is none who has the right to be worshipped but He), the Most Gracious, the Most Merciful.'

(The Qur'aan, Chapter 2: Verse 163)

'Allâh! Lâ ilâha illa Huwa (none has the right to be worshiped but He). And in Allâh (Alone), therefore, let the believers put their trust.'

(The Qur'aan, Chapter 64: Verse 13)

Narrated Mu'adh bin Jabal:

'The Prophet said, "O Mu'adh! Do you know what Allaah's right upon His slaves is?" I said, "Allaah and His Apostle know best." The Prophet said, "To worship Him (Allaah) alone and to join none in worship with Him (Allaah). Do you know what their right upon Him is?" I replied, "Allaah and His Apostle know best." The Prophet said, "Not to punish them (if they do so)."'

(Bukhari Volume 9, Book 93, Number 470)

Narrated Ibn Abbas:

'When the Prophet sent Muadh to Yemen, he said to him, "You are going to a nation from the people of the Scripture, so let the first thing to which you will invite them be the Tawheed of Allaah (to the belief of the Oneness of God the Greatest). If they learn that, tell them that Allaah has enjoined on them five prayers, to be offered in one day and one night. And if they pray, tell them that Allaah has enjoined on them Zakaah (Charity) of their properties and it is to be taken from the rich among them and given to the poor. And if they agree to that, then take from them Zakaah but avoid the best property of the people."'

(Bukhari Volume 9, Book 93, Number 469)

'Surely Allaah alone is the Creator of all things and He is the One, the Most Supreme.'

(The Qur'aan, Chapter 13: Verse 17)

2. ***Believing and obeying the Prophet Muhammad (PBUH):*** That he (PBUH) was the last and final messenger of Allaah (SWT) sent to mankind to guide them to the path of truth and righteousness.

'O you who believe! Believe in Allâh, and His Messenger (Muhammad SAW), and the Book (the Qur'ân) which He has sent down to His Messenger, and the Scripture which He sent down to those before (him), and whosoever disbelieves in Allâh, His Angels, His Books, His Messengers, and the Last Day, then indeed he has strayed far away.'

(The Qur'aan, Chapter 4: Verse 136)

Narrated Ibn 'Umar:

'Allaah's Apostle said: Islam is based on (the following) five (principles):

1. To testify that none has the right to be worshiped but Allaah and Muhammad is Allaah's Apostle.

2. *To offer the (compulsory congregational) prayers dutifully and perfectly.*

3. *To pay Zakaah (obligatory charity).*

4 *To observe the fasts during the month of Ramadhaan.*

5. *To perform Hajj (Pilgrimage to Makkah).*

(Bukhari Volume 1, Book 2, Number 7)

Narrated by Anas:

'*The Prophet said, "Whoever possesses the following three qualities will have the sweetness (delight) of faith:*

1. *The one to whom Allaah and His Apostle becomes dearer than anything else;*

2. *Who loves a person and he loves him only for Allaah's Sake;*

3. *Who hates to revert to atheism (disbelief) as he hates to be thrown into the fire."'*

(Bukhari Volume 1, Book 2, Number 15)

'Muhammad (PBUH) is not the father of any of your men, but he is the Messenger of Allâh and the last (end) of the Prophets. And Allâh is Ever All-Aware of everything.'

(The Qur'aan, Chapter 33: Verse 40)

Although the above (2) Teen Islam Smarts (Obedience of Allaah and the Prophet Muhammad (SAAW)) cover all of the aspects of Teen Islam smarts, below from #3 to #11, I will be mentioning just for more emphasis, inshAllaah.

3. *Offering salaah on time:* Many of us hear this, but imagine that one day we will do it that way. A question to ask yourself is what if you don't have that one day? What if today is your last day? You know that you're accountable to Allaah (SWT) at this age, as a teen. Don't count on tomorrow for tomorrow is not promised to anyone.

Narrated 'Abdullaah:

'I asked the Prophet (PBUH) "Which deed is the dearest to God?" He replied, "To offer the prayers at their early stated fixed times." I asked, "What is the next (in goodness)?" He replied, "To be good and dutiful to your parents."'

(Bukhari)

Abu Hurairah (may Allaah be pleased with him) said:

'The Prophet (may Allaah's Blessings and Peace be upon him) said, "Let anyone tell me; if a stream flows by the house of any person and he baths in it five times a day, whether any dirt will remain on his body?" The companions replied that no dirt would remain in such a case. He said, "So is the case with prescribed prayers. Allaah forgives men's sins (minor) on their account."'

(Bukhari, Muslim)

Allaah (SWT) says in the Qur'aan:

'Verily, As-Salaah (the prayer) is enjoined on the believers at fixed hours.'

(The Qur'aan, Chapter 4: Verse 103)

4. Give charity: Charity is something as simple as a smile. Anything one does that is nice for another could be counted as charity *insha'Allaah*.

"Every act of goodness is charity."

(Muslim)

In fact, Prophet Muhammad told his followers that *sadaqah* (voluntary charity) is incumbent upon them every single day. But this *sadaqah* can take many forms:

"There is a (compulsory) sadaqah (charity) to be given for every joint of the human body (as a sign of gratitude to Allaah) every day the sun rises. To judge justly between two persons is regarded as sadaqah; and to help a man concerning his riding animal, by helping him to mount it or by lifting his luggage on to it, is also regarded as sadaqah; and (saying) a good word is also sadaqah; and every step taken on one's way to offer the compulsory prayer (in the mosque) is also sadaqah; and to remove a harmful thing from the way is also sadaqah."

(Bukhari)

Narrated Jarir bin 'Abdullaah,

'I gave the pledge of allegiance to the Prophet for offering prayer perfectly, giving Zakaah and giving good advice to every Muslim.'

(Bukhari Volume 2, Book 24, Number 484)

Narrated Abu Hurairah:

'Allaah's Apostle said, "Whoever is made wealthy by Allaah and does not pay the Zakaah of his wealth, then on the Day of Resurrection his wealth will be made like a bald-headed poisonous male snake with two black spots over the eyes. The snake will encircle his neck and bite his cheeks and say, 'I am your wealth, I am your treasure.'" Then the Prophet recited the verses:
'Let not those who withhold . . .' (to the end of the verse) (3: 180)

(Bukhari Volume 2, Book 24, Number 486)

'The likeness of those who spend their wealth in the way of Allaah is as the likeness of a grain (of corn) which grows seven ears, and each ear has a hundred grains. Allaah gives manifold increase to whom He pleases. And Allaah is All-Sufficient for His creatures' needs, All-Knower.'

(The Qur'aan, Chapter 2: Verse 261)

5. **Fasting in the month of Ramadhaan:**
Living in the West as well as other parts of the world, many Muslims get used to the culture they were brought up in. I know that in the West people don't fast, some of the religious groups might stay away from certain foods, but

they don't fast like the Muslims do, which is abstaining from food and drink from dawn to sunset. Well, as a teen this actually seems harder, because all day everyone around you is eating, and you have to fast. Many teens have begun lying about fasting just so they don't have to hear the lecture from their family. They will eat in school, but refrain from it at home until sunset. I know because I was raised in America and I saw it happening with my own friends. I was very saddened about this whole ordeal.

What is fasting? Fasting is required of every Muslim who has reached the age of puberty. It has so many benefits that it is unbelievable. While fasting the digestive system relaxes, and it helps manages weight. However for the Muslim, it is beyond health. It is to please the Creator, and to obey Him, and Him alone.

Thus Allaah says in hadith qudsi that

"Fasting is for Me and I only will reward it".

'O you who have believed, decreed upon you is fasting as it was decreed upon those before you that you may become righteous.'

(The Qur'aan, Chapter 2: Verse 183)

6. _Make an account for Hajj:_ Many of you might think I am only a teen; I don't need an account for

Hajj. Let me tell you something; do not depend on anyone else to take you for Hajj. Hajj is obligatory on all that have the means to go there, so start saving for it *insha'Allaah*. My daughter started saving for it since the age of 5, *masha'Allaah*. You can do it too! Just put in a few dollars a week; your change, Eid money, anything, but start saving *insha'Allaah*.

Narrated Abu Hurairah:

'The Prophet (PBUH) said, "Whoever performs Hajj for Allaah's Pleasure and does not have intimate relations with his wife, and does not do evil or sins then he will return (after Hajj free from all sins) as if he were born anew."'

(Bukhari Volume 2, Book 26, Number 596)

Narrated 'Aisha *(The mother of the faithful believers):*

'I said, "O Allaah's Apostle! We consider Jihaad as the best deed." The Prophet said, "The best Jihaad (for women) is Hajj Mabrur."'

(Bukhari Volume 2, Book 26, Number 595)

'And Hajj (pilgrimage to Makkah) to the House (Ka'bah) is a duty that mankind owes to Allaah, those who can afford the expenses.'

(The Qur'aan, Chapter 3: Verse 9)

7. _Respect your parents:_ What I have come to notice is that many people do not respect their parents these days. It is the lifestyle and culture of the West that many are picking up. This is not the Islamic way of life. In Islam after loving and respecting Allaah (SWT) and the Prophet Muhammad (PBUH), then it is your parents that you must respect. Parents are very important; try to give them a hug every day. Try to listen to your parents even when it is hard; you don't have to agree or disagree, just listen to what they say.

'Your Lord has decreed that you worship none but Him, and that you be dutiful to your parents. If one or both of them attain old age in your life, say not to them a word of disrespect, nor shout at them, but address them in terms of honor.'

(The Qur'aan, Chapter 17: Verse 23)

'Be grateful to Me and to your parents; to Me is the [final] destination. But if they endeavor to make you associate with Me that of which you have no knowledge, do not obey them but accompany them in [this] world with

appropriate kindness and follow the way of those who turn back to Me [in repentance]. Then to Me will be your return, and I will inform you about what you used to do.'

(The Qur'aan, Chapter 31: Verse 14-15)

'Anas narrated from Prophet Muhammad about the major sins. He (Muhammed) observed: Associating anyone with God, disobedience to parents, killing a person and false utterance.'

(Muslim)

Narrated by 'Abdullaah:

'I asked the Prophet (PBUH) "Which deed is the dearest to God?" He replied, "To offer the prayers at their early stated fixed times." I asked, "What is the next (in goodness)?" He replied, "To be good and dutiful to your parents."'

(Bukhari)

8. *Have tolerance:* Teen years are when one is most defiant of everything, and one wants to voice their opinions all the time. While it is good to voice your opinions, you still have to pay attention to the situation you are voicing your opinion to, your tone and your attitude.

We can't let situations make us react to them sharply. We need to think about what is happening and then think about how the Prophet Muhammad (PBUH) or the *Sahaabah* (RA) reacted to similar situations in the past.

> *'...who repress anger, and who pardon men; verily, Allaah loves Al-Muhsinun (the good-doers)."*

(The Qur'aan, Chapter 3: Verse 134)

Ibn `Abbas (May Allaah be pleased with them) reported: The Messenger of Allaah (PBUH) said to Ashaj Abdul-Qais (May Allaah be pleased with him),

> *'You possess two qualities that Allaah loves. These are clemency and tolerance.'*

(Muslim)

> *'If anyone harms (others), Allaah will harm him, and if anyone shows hostility to others, Allaah will show hostility to him.'*

(Abu-Dawood, Hadith 1625)

'Aishah (May Allaah be pleased with her) reported:

'The Prophet (PBUH) said, "Allaah is The Forbearer and He loves forbearance in all matters."'

(Bukhari & Muslim)

`Aishah (May Allah be pleased with her) reported: 'The Prophet (PBUH) said,

"Whenever forbearance is added to something, it adorns it; and whenever it is withdrawn from something, it leaves it defective."'

(Muslim)

9. Be patient: Patience is one of the hardest qualities for many people; especially in a day and age where instant gratification is a must. Patience is something that everyone must work on.

Abu Yahya Suhaib bin Sinan (May Allaah be pleased with him) reported that:

'The Messenger of Allaah (PBUH) said, "How wonderful is the case of a believer; there is good for him in everything and this applies only to a believer. If prosperity attends him, he expresses gratitude to Allaah and that is good for him; and if adversity befalls him, he endures it patiently and that is better for him."'

(Muslim)

Abu Hurairah (May Allaah be pleased with him) reported:

'The Messenger of Allaah (PBUH) said, "Allaah, the Exalted, says: 'I have no reward other than Jannah for a believing slave of Mine who remains patient for My sake when I take away his beloved one from among the inhabitants of the world.'"

(Bukhari)

'Verily, man is in loss, except those who believe and do good deeds and encourage one another towards truth and encourage one another towards patience.'

(The Qur'aan, Chapter 104: Verses 2-3)

10. Always make du'aa: Du'aa is the WEAPON of believers. No one can take it away from us. Be consistent, and take time out every day to make *du'aa* to Allaah (SWT). Ask Him what you need help with, what you would like to succeed in, and to forgive you for your weaknesses.

Abu Hurairah (May Allaah be pleased with him) reported: 'The Messenger of Allaah (PBUH) said:

"The supplication of every one of you will be granted if he does not get impatient and say

(for example): `I supplicated my Rabb but my prayer has not been granted'."'

(Bukhari and Muslim)

'"Any Muslim who supplicates to Allaah in a du'aa, which contains no sin nor breaking of family ties, Allaah will give him one of three things: either his du`aa will be immediately answered or, it will be saved for him in the hereafter, or it will turn away an equivalent amount of evil (from him)." The companions said "So we will ask for more." He replied, "Allaah is More Generous."'

(At-Tirmidhi, Ahmad)

'And your Lord said: Invoke Me [i.e. believe in My Oneness (Islamic Monotheism)] (and ask Me for anything) I will respond to your invocation.'
(The Qur'aan, Chapter 40: Verse 60)

11. _Never oppress:_ This is a hot topic. Islam does not oppress, nor should you as a teen do it. Many times I get asked the question, how can a teen oppress, they don't have any power? Teens oppress in a different manner than adults or leaders. Oppression has many forms; it could be with one's tongue, one's actions, and could even involve getting others to do it.

Narrated Abu Said Al-Khudri:

'Allaah's Apostle said, "When the believers pass safely over (the bridge across) Hell, they will be stopped at a bridge in-between Hell and Paradise where they will retaliate upon each other for the injustices done among them in the world, and when they get purified of all their sins, they will be admitted into Paradise. By Him in Whose Hands the life of Muhammad is everybody will recognize his dwelling in Paradise better than he recognizes his dwelling in this world."'

(Bukhari Volume 3, Book 43, Number 620)

Narrated 'Abdullaah bin Umar:

'Allaah's Apostle said, "A Muslim is a brother of another Muslim, so he should not oppress him, nor should he hand him over to an oppressor. Whoever fulfilled the needs of his brother, Allaah will fulfill his needs; whoever brought his (Muslim) brother out of a discomfort, Allaah will bring him out of the discomforts of the Day of Resurrection, and whoever screened a Muslim, Allaah will screen him on the Day of Resurrection."

(Bukhari Volume 3, Book 43, Number 622)

'And as for those who emigrated for the Cause of Allâh, after suffering oppression, We will certainly give them goodly residence in this world, but indeed the reward of the Hereafter will be greater, if they but knew!'

(The Qur'aan, Chapter 16: Verse 41)

If you can memorize and act upon these ten 'Teen Islam Smarts', *insha'Allaah* you're on your way to success. Please post these ten 'Teen Islam Smarts' everywhere, so that you can remember them often, *insha'Allaah*.

Activity to do

1. Who are you?

2. What do you dream of wanting to become?

3. What decision will you make right now to help increase your learning?

Chapter

5

Teen Leadership

'A great leader is one who is successful in achieving success in this world, as well as the hereafter insha'Allaah.'

Zohra Sarwari

'When three men travel together, they should make one of them their leader.'

(Abu Dawood, on the authority of Abu Sa'id 'Al-Khudri)

Ten Qualities Every Great Teen Leader Must Possess

1. Be a Visionary

Your vision must be crystal clear. This is the vision that teens must have; what is it that you want to accomplish? It must be crystal clear if you want to lead. How can you lead others if you don't know where you're headed? A leader sees the big picture and then makes a plan to get there, *insha'Allaah*. As a leader give simple steps, to help achieve your vision. Remember that teens don't follow teens, they follow the vision that they are working towards.

2. Be a Role-Model

Do you know that 80% of teens learn from observing other teens and adults? As the old saying goes, *"Walk the walk, and talk the talk."* Nowadays, what people tell others to do, they don't do it themselves. They don't 'practice what they preach.' Many times I notice a leader promoting weight loss and yet she can't control herself. This isn't being a role model. No one is perfect but if you're a leader, you must try to 'practice what you preach.'

> *'O you who believe! Why do you say that which you do not do?'*

> **(The Qur'aan, Chapter 61: Verse 2)**

3. Be Action-Oriented

You might have heard many people say, *'I want to do this or I want to go to this college'*, but yet they never take any action to make it happen. A leader is someone who takes ACTION; one who is doing, not just talking. They know that certain decisions might make them fail, but failure is not going to stop them from acting. It doesn't matter if they don't get into a certain university; the fact that they applied shows that they have a chance.

> *'And say (O Muhammad SAW) "Do deeds! Allâh will see your deeds, and (so will) His*

Messenger and the believers. And you will be brought back to the All-Knower of the unseen and the seen. Then He will inform you of what you used to do."'

(The Qur'aan, Chapter 9: Verse 105)

4. Be Intuitive

Listen to your gut feeling when it tells you to stop or go on. When you have a gut feeling about it, this is one of those instances when a leader should pray the *istikhaarah*; always depend on Allaah (SWT) for any decision.

You usually know if something is right or wrong when you're doing it. If you don't, and your gut feeling is telling you that you're doing something wrong, look into it. Always ask an elder or a more knowledgeable person who you trust, and get a few opinions. Great leaders always have mentors. Every decision is inspected to make sure it is the correct decision, *insha'Allaah*.

5. Have Integrity

Be one person; be the same you on the inside as you are on the outside. Many leaders today are one way at home and with their close personal friends, and then a different way with others. As a teen, many of you are still discovering who you are; find who you are and be one you; be your best, and don't be fake. Just be you; the same you that Allaah (SWT) Sees 24 hours a day.

'Virtue is noble behavior, and sin is that which creates doubt and you do not like people to know about it.'

(Muslim)

6. Be Passionate

The leaders must be passionate about their project; it is their energy which will bring other people into the limelight. They must be excited about what they are leading. It is passion for their vision that will inspire others to get excited and join.

7. Be Competent

A leader must be skilled in the area he or she is leading; they must possess knowledge, skills and the ability to interact with others. Often people have knowledge or skills but they lack communication skills. Communication skills are a must; he or she must know how to relay his/her message to their team.

'Whoever delegates a position to someone whereas he sees someone else as more competent (for the position); verily he has cheated Allaah and His Apostle and all the Muslims.'

(Ibn Taymiyyah, Assiyasah Ash-Shar'iyya 1996)

8. Be Compassionate

A leader must be compassionate towards everyone he or she deals with. This is a quality many leaders lack today. Even if you don't agree with something or someone, or something gets you upset, show compassion; always put yourself in the other person's shoes. This can make it easier to have compassion; by thinking of what they are going through.

'It is better for a leader to make a mistake in forgiving than to make a mistake in punishing.'

(Al-Tirmidhi, Hadith 1011)

'None of you (truly) believes, until he wishes for his brother what he wishes for himself.'

(Bukhari)

9. Have Courage

Leaders must face fear in the face; everyone has fears, but as a teen leader you must manage your fears and move ahead, even though you're afraid. Teen leaders must be courageous, but also be ready to admit their mistakes. It takes courage to admit you have made a mistake but it takes more courage to learn from that mistake and try not to do it again *insha'Allaah*.

10. Always Keep Learning

A leader should always be willing to learn, *insha'Allaah*. This helps to expand your mind and grow. Read through books of biographies; start with the biography of the Prophet Muhammad (PBUH) and then read the Sahaabah's biographies. You will see what type of leaders they were, where they made their mistakes and the wisdom behind the way they worked as a team. After reading these biographies, read biographies of other leaders who have made a difference; and learn from them *insha'Allaah*. Always remember as you're learning that you're obeying Allaah (SWT) first and foremost. A lot of things that different leaders do, we might not accept in Islam. Some leaders have tortured their enemies at their hands and that is not a teaching of Islam; know your values as a leader.

From Jaabir (RA) who said that Allâh's Messenger (PBUH) said:

'Do not acquire knowledge in order to compete with the scholars, nor to argue with the ignorant, nor to gain mastery over the gatherings. Since whoever does that, then: The Fire! The Fire!'

(*Abu Dawood No. 3656*)

Activity to do

1. What are two leadership qualities that you
    would like to work on for yourself?

    ----

2. How will you work on them?

Have You Booked
"The Most Inspirational Muslim Woman Speaker In America?"

Zohra Sarwari

An Inspiring and Motivating Speaker for Your Next Event!

"Zohra Sarwari has a great skill for making you want to achieve on a higher level. Your students will enjoy learning from her!"

Jonathan Sprinkles
Former APCA National College 'Speaker of the Year'
www.jsprinkles.com

"After hearing Zohra Sarwari's speech, I was profoundly moved by her enthusiasm to further educate me on the way the Muslims live. Her knowledge instilled a greater understanding and appreciation in me."

Debbie Burke
High School Teacher
Indianapolis, Indiana

www.zohrasarwari.com

"Zohra Sarwari has stood out as exceptionally creative and extraordinarily passionate about her topics. Her energy is contagious."

Muhammad Alshareef
President, AlMaghrib Institute

"Zohra's effort should be viewed in two disciplines. The first discipline is that we seek a destiny that befits our quality of life. The second discipline is that we seek a destiny to befit the quality of earning in our lives. She has carefully crafted a dialogue of addressing our spiritual, emotional, and financial roadblocks. This book is a win-win for those don't win enough, and for those who may not have won at all. Embrace the book, begin your journey."

Preacher Moss
Founder of "Allah Made me Funny"
The Official Muslim Comedy Tour

Interested in other products by Zohra? Take a look at what she has to offer:

9 Steps To Achieve Your Destiny
Become the Change that You Envision in this World

9 Steps To Achieve Your Destiny explores the steps that, if practiced daily, will change your life God-Willing. It shows you how your thinking and habits can make you either successful or stagnant, and helps you navigate your way to right choices and productive habits.

Imagine That Today is Your Last Day
How would you be if you knew that today was the last day of your life?

Imagine That Today is Your Last Day reveals to you the secrets of living a great life and accepting your fate when it arrives. The book discusses the missing link in your life for which you will have to pay a price after death. Bring every moment to life, it can be your LAST day TODAY! It is an experience that many never think about, let alone go through it.

NO! I AM NOT A TERRORIST!

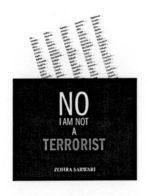

'Terrorism' and 'terrorist' are the latest media buzzwords! However, do you actually know what each of these terms mean? Do you know who a 'terrorist' is? What comes to your mind when you think of a 'terrorist'? Is it a man with a beard, or is it a woman in a veil? Muslims worldwide are being stereotyped and labeled as 'terrorists'. Have you ever stopped and wondered why? Have you ever made the time to discover what lies under the beard and the dress? Have you ever stopped to think what Islam actually has to say about 'terrorism'? Find the answers to all the above questions and more in this book, 'NO! I AM NOT A TERRORIST!'

Are Muslim Women Oppressed?

Are Muslim Women OPPRESSED?

ZOHRA SARWARI

Learn about the dignified and well-managed lives of Muslim women and know the reasons why they dress the way they do. 'Are Muslim Women OPPRESSED?' answers your questions: Why do Muslim women wear those weird clothes? Are they doing it for men? Are they inferior? Do they have no rights? 'Are Muslim Women OPPRESSED?' will reveal the truth behind the concealed Muslim woman. It is a voyage from behind the veil to the real freedom and will give you an insight about Muslim women like you have never read before. Read and clear the misconceptions; separate the facts from the myths!